Homemade Cat Treats

Put the Meow Back into Their Food

BY: Ivy Hope

Copyright © 2020 by Ivy Hope

Copyright/License Page

Please don't reproduce this book. It means you are not allowed to make any type of copy (print or electronic), sell, publish, disseminate or distribute. Only people who have written permission from the author are allowed to do so.

This book is written by the author taking all precautions that the content is true and helpful. However, the reader needs to be careful about his/her action. If anything happens due to the reader's actions the author won't be taken as responsible.

Table of Contents

Introduction 6

Homemade Cat Foods 8

    Tuna Patties 9

    Salmon Yummy 11

    Sardine Meal 13

    Homemade Cat Stew 15

    Chicken Cat Food 17

    Easy Tuna Recipe 19

    Homemade Breakfast for The Cat 21

    Canned Homemade Cat Food 23

    Homemade Fish Recipe 25

    Homemade Lamb Cat Food 27

    Homemade Dry Cat Food 29

    Homemade Vegetarian Dish for Cats 31

    Homemade Turkey and Fish Recipe 33

Homemade Ground Beef Cat Food 35

Homemade Pasta Recipe for Cats 37

Homemade Cat Treats 39

Moe's Favorite Treats 40

Homemade Salmon and Sweet Potato Cat Treats 42

Homemade Cheese Cat Treats 44

Homemade Sardines Cookies 46

Homemade Frozen Banana Cat Pops 48

Homemade Catnip Treats 50

Homemade Tuna and Cheddar Cat Treats 52

Easy Homemade Salmon Treats 54

Homemade Spinach and Chicken Cat Treats 56

Homemade Cat Cookies 58

Homemade Liver Treats 60

Homemade Pumpkin Cat Treats 62

Homemade Cat Pudding Recipe 64

Homemade Grain-Free Cat Treats 66

Homemade Cat Bruschetta 68

About the Author 70

Author's Afterthoughts 71

Introduction

Actually, cats can be very finicky when it comes to their food. Making homemade food can be trial and error for you and your cat. Trying different combinations of food and giving it to your cat will be the best way to make the ones he/she likes.

Store bought cat foods can include ingredients that are not that good for your feline. You have to be careful about the ash content in cat food. If too much is in it, your cat may suffer from urinary tract infections. Just be careful when buying store bought.

One way to solve it is to make your own cat food. Choose the ingredients that are good for your cat and cook away. Proteins are good starters for cats. Chicken, lean beef, liver, lamb or eggs will provide good protein when making homemade cat foods. Snacks may include some vegetables such as

Pumpkin, peas, cucumbers, spinach, cooked carrots, cooked broccoli, cooked green beans and asparagus are good ones to use. You can add grains such as corn, bread and oatmeal. Fruits are not always a favorite of cats, but if they like it, you can use, bananas, watermelon, apples and blueberries.

Cheese and yogurt can be used also. Canned tuna and salmon can be used as well as fish oil.

Your cat will love you for making his favorite foods and snacks. Gather the ingredients and start cooking.

Homemade Cat Foods

Tuna Patties

Actually, this is one of the easiest recipes to make. It contains wholesome ingredients that will leave your cat meowing for more.

Prep Time: 10 minutes

Yields: 7 patties

Ingredients:

- Tuna, 1 can, drained
- Rice, ½ cup, boiled
- Liver, ¼ cup, pureed
- Parsley, 2 sprigs, chopped

Directions:

1. Combine all the ingredients.

2. Form into 7 patties and store in refrigerator.

3. Serve to cat when ready.

Salmon Yummy

There are not very many cats that do not love salmon. This is a great one to keep on hand. Be sure and use before 3 days, while it is fresh.

Prep Time: 20 minutes

Yields: 1 ½ cups

Ingredients:

- Salmon, 1 can, drained
- Broccoli, 1 tbsp., cooked and mashed
- Whole Wheat Breadcrumbs, ¼ cup
- Brewer's Yeast, 1 tsp.

Directions:

1. Mix the salmon, broccoli, breadcrumbs and yeast.

2. Combine well and serve.

3. Lastly, store in refrigerator for up to 3 days.

Sardine Meal

I do not like sardines, but my cat loves them. My husband enjoys them too. This is another quick and easy meal to fix for your finicky cat.

Prep Time: 15 minutes

Yields: 1 ½ cups

Ingredients:

- Salmon, 1 can in oil
- Carrot, 2 tbsp., grated
- Oatmeal, 1/3 cup, cooked

Directions:

1. Mix salmon, carrot and oatmeal together.

2. Squish together and serve to your cat.

3. Store in refrigerator up to 3 days.

Homemade Cat Stew

This is a cat meal that humans can consume. The ingredients will be great in the stew. You have to like a rabbit, though. Not everyone does.

Prep Time: 30 minutes

Yields: 4 cups

Ingredients:

- Rabbit, 1 lb., cut into small pieces
- Olive Oil, 1 tbsp.
- Parsley, 2 sprigs, chopped
- Vegetable Stock, 15 oz.
- Sweet Potato, 1 chopped
- Carrot, 1 chopped
- Celery, 1 stalk, chopped
- Turnip, 1 small, chopped
- Peas, 1 cup

Directions:

1. Brown rabbit in the oil.

2. Remove and add to crock pot

3. Add the rest of the ingredients and set to high.

4. Cook for 3 to 4 hrs., until rabbit is tender.

5. Turn off and serve.

Chicken Cat Food

Chicken is a great one to use. Even finicky cats enjoy chicken. It is versatile with ingredients and makes it easy for good combinations.

Prep Time: 30 minutes

Yields: 1 ½ cups

Ingredients:

- Chicken, 1 cup, cooked and chopped
- Rice, ½ cup, cooked
- Broccoli, ½ cup, cooked and chopped
- Carrot, ¼ cup, cooked and chopped
- Chicken Broth, 1 cup

Directions:

1. Combine the chicken, rice, broccoli and carrot in blender and process.

2. Add the broth until it is held together.

3. Dish out and serve.

Easy Tuna Recipe

This one is basically combine and serve recipe.

Prep Time: 15 minutes

Yields: 1 cup

Ingredients:

- Tuna, 1 can, in water
- Carrots, ½ cup, cooked and chopped
- Canola Oil, 1 tsp.
- Egg, 1 hard boiled, chopped

Directions:

1. Combine all of the ingredients together.

2. Mix well and serve.

3. Store rest in refrigerator for up to 2 days.

Homemade Breakfast for The Cat

We can eat breakfast, so can your cats. This yummy dish will delight them. Most cats are more than ready to eat in the morning. Have this on hand for them.

Prep Time: 20 minutes

Serves: 1 omelet

Ingredients:

- Nonfat dry milk, 1 tbsp.
- Eggs, 3 medium
- Cottage Cheese, 3 tbsp.
- Veggies of choice, 2 tbsp., grated
- Oil, 1 tsp.

Directions:

1. Combine the milk and eggs with water.

2. Cook in oil as you would an omelet.

3. Add the cottage cheese and veggies once you flip the egg.

4. Fold and chop into small pieces for your cat.

Canned Homemade Cat Food

This is a great idea to keep this recipe on hand. You can save for a long time and serve when best suited for your cat. This is also a yummy recipe for them. Just save the insides from your chicken and turkey to make this.

Prep Time: 30 minutes

Yields: 10 small jars

Ingredients:

- Liver, ½ lb.
- Gizzards, ½ lb.
- Hearts, ½ lb.
- Wheat Bread, 2 slices
- Rice, 1 cup, cooked

Directions:

1. Boil the liver, gizzards and hearts until done. Run through meat grinder.

2. Combine the above ingredients with the bread and rice.

3. Pour into small jars, then pressure cook as you would in canning.

4. Store in cabinet when finished.

Homemade Fish Recipe

The ingredients are healthy and wholesome. Make sure you check with your vet that a special diet does not need to be left. Once you get the ok, start cooking.

Prep Time: 30 minutes

Yields: 6 cups

Ingredients:

- Mackerel fillets, 1 ½ lb.
- Green beans, ½ lb., chopped
- Kelp powder, 1 tbsp.
- Carrots, ½ lb., chopped
- Celery, ½ lb. chopped
- Water, 6 cups

Directions:

1. Mix all the ingredients above and simmer.

2. Puree the mixture after it is done.

3. Pour in containers and store in refrigerator up to two days.

Homemade Lamb Cat Food

Lamb is delicious any way it is prepared. I do not usually use lamb in my recipes due to the expense. Certainly, I do splurge every once in a while, and make this delicious meal for them.

Prep Time: 30 minutes

Yields: 1 cup

Ingredients:

- Lamb, 1 cup, ground
- Brown rice, ½ cup, cooked
- Alfalfa sprouts, 6 tbsp., minced
- Cottage Cheese, ¾ cup, small curd

Directions:

1. Brown the lamb and cool when done.

2. Combine with rice, cottage cheese and sprouts.

3. Serve and store the remainder in refrigerator up to 2 days.

Homemade Dry Cat Food

Dry cat food can also be made at home. At least you know what goes into it. Your cats can nibble on this for several days.

Prep Time: 30 minutes

Yields: 6 to 8 cups

Ingredients:

- Cornmeal, 1 cup
- Soy flour, 2 cups
- Whole wheat flour, 3 cups
- Wheat germ, 1 cup
- Mackerel, 1 can
- Cd liver oil, 5 tbsp.
- Fat free milk, 1 cup
- Brewer's yeast, ½ cup
- Water, 2 cups

Directions:

1. Combine cornmeal, flours, yeast and wheat germ.

2. Combine the mashed mackerel, oil, water and milk.

3. Mix the two together and form dough.

4. Roll out flat and cut into small pieces.

5. Bake for 25 minutes in 350' oven.

6. Store in refrigerator.

Homemade Vegetarian Dish for Cats

Sometimes a vegetarian dish is good for all. Combine all the ingredients and serve. The catnip will lure the cat in for sure.

Prep Time: 20 minutes

Yields: ½ cup

Ingredients:

- Catnip, ¼ tsp.
- Alfalfa sprouts, ½ cup, chopped
- Zucchini, ¼ cup, grated
- Fish stock, 1/8 cup

Directions:

1. Mix the sprouts and zucchini together.

2. Add the stock and combine well. Sprinkle with catnip.

3. Serve to kitty and watch the enjoyment.

Homemade Turkey and Fish Recipe

Fish and turkey are two ingredients my cat loves. He waits for it when it is cooking, looking at me the whole time. I know his mouth is watering, so he will love this recipe.

Prep Time: 20 minutes

Yields: 1 cup

Ingredients:

- Turkey, ½ cup, cooked
- Tuna, 1 can in oil
- Carrot, 1 tbsp., cooked and mashed
- Brown rice, 2 tbsp. cooked

Directions:

1. Combine all of the ingredients in blender and puree.

2. Serve to your cat when finished.

3. If any left, store in refrigerator up to 2 days.

Homemade Ground Beef Cat Food

Ground beef is not one of my cat's favorite, but he will eat it. However, my dog will devour what he does not eat, so I cook a meal for both.

Prep Time: 45 minutes

Yields: 1 bowl

Ingredients:

- Ground beef, ½ lb.
- Rice, ¼ cup
- Egg, 1 hard-boiled
- Olive Oil, 4 tsps.
- Chicken Stock, 1 cup

Directions:

1. Combine all the ingredients and cook on medium heat for 20 minutes.

2. Add to blender and mix.

3. Serve to kitty then store the rest in the refrigerator for no more than 2 days.

Homemade Pasta Recipe for Cats

Chicken and pasta are a great dish for the cats. I like it too! However, my cat may not let me have any. It will be a winner with the cats.

Prep Time: 20 minutes

Yields: 2 cups

Ingredients:

- Ground Chicken, ½ lb.
- Carrot, 1 small, chopped
- Macaroni, ½ cup
- Vegetable Oil, 2 tbsp.
- Chicken Stock, 1 ½ cups

Directions:

1. Cook the chicken in the oil until done.

2. Combine the chicken, stock, carrot and macaroni.

3. Once boiling, turn down. Then, simmer for 15 minutes.

4. Cool mixture, then mash together in blender.

5. Serve, then store remainder in refrigerator for up to 2 days.

Homemade Cat Treats

Moe's Favorite Treats

Moe is a very finicky cat. He likes his treats, but only certain flavors. Anything fishy is a winner with him. He sometimes eats chicken and beef, but fish is his favorite.

Prep Time: 30 minutes

Yields: 4 cups

Ingredients:

- Tuna, 1 can, in water
- Flour, 1 cup
- Cornmeal, 1 cup
- Vegetable Oil, ½ cup
- Water, ¼ cup
- Salt, ¼ tsp.

Directions:

1. Combine all of the above ingredients together.

2. Make a dough and roll it out to ¼ inch thick.

3. Cut into tiny bite-size squares.

4. Bake at 350' for 15 minutes.

5. Store in airtight container.

Homemade Salmon and Sweet Potato Cat Treats

These treats will be acceptable to all cats. The mixture of salmon and sweet potato is a tempting treat for all cats. They can be stored in your refrigerator for 3 days.

Prep Time: 20 minutes

Yields: 40 treats

Ingredients:

- Salmon, 1 can
- Sweet Potato, 1 ½ cups, baked and mashed
- Old-fashioned Oats, 1 ½ cup
- Parsley, ¼ cup

Directions:

1. Mix the salmon and sweet potato together.

2. Grind oats and parsley until fine.

3. Mix everything together and add to a mold of your choice.

4. Freeze until set.

5. Serve and store the rest.

Homemade Cheese Cat Treats

Make the best treats for your cat that you can. Cheese is a favorite of cats. This treat will have them lined up waiting for them.

Prep Time: 30 minutes

Yields: 30 to 40 treats

Ingredients:

- Cheddar Cheese, ¾ cup, shredded
- Parmesan Cheese, 2 tbsp., grated
- Romano Cheese, 2 tbsp., grated
- Plain Yogurt, ¼ cup
- All-purpose Flour, ½ cup
- Wheat Flour, ¼ cup
- Cornmeal, ¼ cup
- Water, ¼ cup

Directions:

1. Mix all of the above ingredients together to form dough.

2. Roll dough out on parchment paper lined cookie sheet.

3. Bake at 350' for 15 minutes or until hard.

4. Remove from parchment paper and cut.

5. Store in container.

Homemade Sardines Cookies

These treats enhance your cat's nutrition and health. They make a big batch and they are very easy to make. Give the sardines a new recipe.

Prep Time: 30 minutes

Yields: 50 treats

Ingredients:

- Sardines, 1 ¾ oz
- Wheat Flour, ½ cup
- Flax seed, 2 tbsp.
- Parsley, ¼ cup
- Egg, 1
- Coconut Oil, 2 tsp.

Directions:

1. Mix the parsley, flour and flax seed together.

2. Blend the sardines, egg and oil until pureed.

3. Mix the flour mixture with the pureed mixture.

4. Form ball with the dough, then roll out flat.

5. Next, place on cookie sheet lined with parchment paper.

6. Bake at 350' for 12 minutes.

7. Cut into small squares when done.

8. Store for up to a month.

Homemade Frozen Banana Cat Pops

Popsicles are a good treat for your cat, when it is made with fresh fruit. Other ingredients can be used to make these frozen treats. They will enjoy them.

Prep Time: 20 minutes

Yields: 12 cubes

Ingredients:

- Cat Milk, 1-6 oz. container
- Bananas, 1 ½ smashed

Directions:

1. Combine the milk and banana. Mix well.

2. Pour mixture into regular ice tray.

3. Freeze in the freezer until used.

4. Store remainder in the freezer.

Homemade Catnip Treats

The love of catnip is engrained in every cat. They tend to go wild for it. Think about how much fun they will have eating these treats! I wonder if it is like marijuana brownies for adults?

Prep Time: 20 minutes

Yields: 30 Treats

Ingredients:

- Tuna, 5 oz., drained
- Egg, 1
- Flour, ½ cup
- Wheat Germ, ¼ cup
- Cornmeal, ½ cup
- Wheat flour, ¼ cup
- Water, 2/3 cup
- Catnip, ½ tbsp.

Directions:

1. Combine all of the ingredients and roll dough into a ball.

2. Roll into balls and place on parchment lined cookie sheet.

3. Bake at 350' for 20 minutes.

4. Cool when finished, then serve.

5. Store in airtight container.

Homemade Tuna and Cheddar Cat Treats

Cheddar and tuna go hand in hand. I have purchased treats made out of these two ingredients. They seem to impress my cat. He always comes back for more.

Prep Time: 20 minutes

Yields: 30 to 40 treats

Ingredients:

- Tuna, 5 oz., drained
- Cheddar Cheese, 1/3 cup, shredded
- Egg, 1
- Oat Flour, 1 1/3 cups
- Catnip, 1 tbsp.
- Cold Water, ½ cup

Directions:

1. Combine tuna and cheddar and blend until fine.

2. Combine the egg, flour, catnip and water and mix with tuna and cheddar mixture.

3. Form dough and roll into a ball.

4. Pull and form small balls and place on cookie pan.

5. Bake at 350' for 15 minutes.

6. These can be store up to a week in the refrigerator.

Easy Homemade Salmon Treats

This is an easy recipe consisting of 3 ingredients. Salmon is always a favorite to use in any cat recipe. It will be requested more and more.

Prep Time: 15 minutes

Yields: 120 Treats

Ingredients:

- Salmon, 10 oz. can, drained
- Egg, 1, beaten
- Wheat Flour, 2 cups

Directions:

1. Chop the salmon until fine.

2. Combine the salmon, egg and flour and blend well.

3. Form dough and roll out flat.

4. Cook with cookie cutter and place on lined cookie sheet.

5. Bake at 350' for 20 minutes.

6. Can store in container for 2 weeks.

Homemade Spinach and Chicken Cat Treats

The catnip included in this recipe will insure your cat will love these treats. They are healthy and you can relax knowing what ingredients are in the treat.

Prep Time: 20 minutes

Yields: 1 ½ cup

Ingredients:

- Chicken thighs, ½ lb. boneless and skinless
- Spinach, 1 cup
- Quick Oats, 1 cup
- Egg, 1
- Catnip, 1 tbsp.
- Flour, ¼ cup

Directions:

1. Cook the chicken, remove and cool.

2. Process the chicken, spinach, oats, egg and catnip in a food processor.

3. Remove and add flour.

4. Form into dough ball and roll out.

5. Cut into small squares or shapes and place on lined cookie sheet.

6. Bake at 350' for 20 minutes.

7. Serve to your cat.

Homemade Cat Cookies

This is a two-ingredient cat treat. Using the pate style of cat food, you just add fish or chicken, then bake. Easy as pie. They will love it.

Prep Time: 10 minutes

Yields: 6 cookies

Ingredients:

- Liver Pate Cat Food, 1 large can
- Freeze dried Fish, 1 small package

Directions:

1. Combine the pate and fish together.

2. Form the patties and place on lined cookie sheet.

3. Bake at 250' for 2 hours.

4. Serve when done.

Homemade Liver Treats

Liver is a favorite for some cats. They will enjoy the treats more than the cat food. The treats smell salty, which a lot of the treats that are store bought smell that way.

Prep Time: 30 minutes

Yields: 18 squares

Ingredients:

- Whole Wheat Flour, ½ cup
- Eggs, 2
- Beef Liver, 1 ½ lb. cut into pieces

Directions:

1. Combine the liver, eggs and flour into food process and chop fine.

2. Mix well, then pour into prepared pan.

3. Bake at 350' for 15 to 20 minutes.

4. When done, cut in small squares.

5. Store in refrigerator.

Homemade Pumpkin Cat Treats

Pumpkin is used a lot to help with constipation in cats. This ingredient will add taste and do a healthy job with digestion.

Prep Time: 30 minutes

Yields: 18 treats

Ingredients:

- Oat Flour, 1 cup
- Catnip, 1 tsp.
- Olive Oil, 1 ½ tsp.
- Pumpkin, ½ cup
- Carrot, 1 cup shredded
- Egg, 1

Directions:

1. Combine all ingredients and beat until dough forms.

2. Spread on floured surface.

3. Cut into shapes and bake at 350' for 15 minutes.

4. Let cool when finished and serve.

Homemade Cat Pudding Recipe

This may be used for kittens, sick cats or cats on restricted diets. It is easy for them to lap it up. They will enjoy this treat and be helped at the same time.

Prep Time: 30 minutes

Yields: 4 puddings

Ingredients:

- Gelatin, 1 cup, unflavored
- Water, 1 ½ cups
- Milk, 1 cup, evaporated
- Yolks, 1
- Mayo, 1 tsp.
- Yogurt, 1 tbsp.
- Corn Syrup, 1 tbsp.

Directions:

1. Combine the gelatin and boiling water to dissolve.

2. Add the remaining ingredients.

3. Pour into 4 small containers and refrigerate until firm.

4. The remainder will last for 1 week.

Homemade Grain-Free Cat Treats

Some cats are allergic to grains just like humans are. It is easy to make these treats without the grains. The consistency will still be a bite-size snack they will love.

Prep Time: 15 minutes

Yields: 24 squares

Ingredients:

- Tuna, 1 can, drained
- Potato Flakes, ½ cup

Directions:

1. Mash tuna and potato flakes together to form dough.

2. Pour into prepared dish.

3. Bake at 350' for 30 minutes.

4. Remove and cut into squares.

5. Can store for up to 2 weeks.

Homemade Cat Bruschetta

The elegance of bruschetta for your favorite cat is an ideal treat for a special cat. Fine dining for our cats is no expense to us.

Prep Time: 15 minutes

Yields: 1 serving

Ingredients:

- Bread, 1 slice
- Fish Oil, 1 tbsp.
- Fish Flakes, 2 tbsp.

Directions:

1. Toast the bread in oven.

2. Brush with fish oil and sprinkle with fish flakes.

3. Cut into cubes and place on baking sheet.

4. Bake at 350' until browned.

5. Cool and serve.

About the Author

Ivy's mission is to share her recipes with the world. Even though she is not a professional cook she has always had that flair toward cooking. Her hands create magic. She can make even the simplest recipe tastes superb. Everyone who has tried her food has astounding their compliments was what made her think about writing recipes.

She wanted everyone to have a taste of her creations aside from close family and friends. So, deciding to write recipes was her winning decision. She isn't interested in popularity, but how many people have her recipes reached and touched people. Each recipe in her cookbooks is special and has a special meaning in her life. This means that each recipe is created with attention and love. Every ingredient carefully picked, every combination tried and tested.

Her mission started on her birthday about 9 years ago, when her guests couldn't stop prizing the food on the table. The next thing she did was organizing an event where chefs from restaurants were tasting her recipes. This event gave her the courage to start spreading her recipes.

She has written many cookbooks and she is still working on more. There is no end in the art of cooking; all you need is inspiration, love, and dedication.

Author's Afterthoughts

I am thankful for downloading this book and taking the time to read it. I know that you have learned a lot and you had a great time reading it. Writing books is the best way to share the skills I have with your and the best tips too.

I know that there are many books and choosing my book is amazing. I am thankful that you stopped and took time to decide. You made a great decision and I am sure that you enjoyed it.

I will be even happier if you provide honest feedback about my book. Feedbacks helped by growing and they still do. They help me to choose better content and new ideas. So, maybe your feedback can trigger an idea for my next book.

Thank you again

Sincerely

Ivy Hope

Printed in Great Britain
by Amazon